**Suffolk Co**

Libraries &

You may keep this title until the last
given on your receipt.
Providing it has not been reserve
may renew it by visiting any Suffolk
or by telephone. To renew
http://libcat.suffolkcc.gov.uk
To renew your loans by telephone, please dial ne
card and (numeric)

BABY

POEMS ON PREGNANCY, BIRTH AND BABIES

Gillian K. Ferguson

CANONGATE

First published in Great Britain in 2001 by
Canongate Books Ltd, 14 High Street, Edinburgh EH1 1TE

10 9 8 7 6 5 4 3 2

The author would like to express her extreme gratitude to the Scottish Arts
Council for its generous assistance – for the writer's bursary which enabled her
to write this book, and in particular for the special support of Jenny Brown,
Director of Literature.

British Library Cataloguing-in-Publication Data
A catalogue record for this book is available on request from the
British Library

ISBN 1 84195 121 8

Typeset by Patty Rennie Production, Glenbervie
Printed and bound by Creative Print and Design, Ebbw Vale, Wales

www.canongate.net

CONTENTS

NEW HUMAN
Puzzled by light, air, touch, love

A BABY
This hand, Bonsai, clutches my heart

BEING HUMAN IS ENOUGH IN COMMON
Fat, Christmas, and ghosts of nightgown

FAMILY AND THE WORLD
Green spring fists, tooth buds and sleeping bees

For my baby, Comrie

A NOISE AMONG THE STARS

Before the beginning, baby hunger, egg and sperm

The Baby Hunger

When did the baby hunger begin?
When bald, bawling, nappy-loaded,
puking bairns that other grown up
people had like tame aliens became
the only thing possible to fill a hole
in my stomach the size of the world,
and the need to feel small fingers
in mine made me feel mad. Tragic.

Not even a man, and as magazines
advise, let on and he'll run a mile –
if he's even born, in the same hemisphere.

When did children begin to loom
from the landscape, step from
the scenery, with faces. To toddle
into my dreams wearing my hair,
looking at me with my eyes miniaturised.

When did the park start to make me sad,
a torture of families hysterically picnicking,
pregnant friends in the club disappear
into opaque experience, double-glazed.

Not one day or the next, when the mess
of blood and egg seemed such a waste,
and pain not just in the pelvic cavity.
Maybe at the end of the twenty started
years, as if the earth turning slowly
began to see the moon.

There should be a Noise

There should be a noise among the stars,
their light should clang together like silver bells,
a disturbance of fish in the ocean; whales and
shark, dolphin, shaken, composing new songs.

The sun should appear from cloud like an eye
from a lid, look full on the moon, melt white
silence into brooding music, vault Poles, ring
icicles like rutting unicorns, gild black birds

breeding air and wing. Sky should snap suddenly
blue like a kingfisher, open as a mouth from the
horizon, to sing. There should be fever in the earth,
stones boiling into hills; rain must explain with

million finger Morse. Crowds of snowflakes should
panic down, babbling, dancing on roofs their crystal
patterns, high as piccolos. Wind in the world's throat
needs tongues of trees, language of leaves; is silenced

by space. How can night's black lips slip shut
at the horizon slit, and the trumpeting morning
be deaf to God's sigh of satisfaction, the shudder
in the universe at the sound of sperm penetrating egg.

Sperm on Legs

Says Jean – 'It's terrible, I don't see men any more,
just sperm on legs. I'm dreaming of his genes,
never mind his butt in jeans. Designer brands,

I no longer care; does he know Levi-Strauss,
Claude, not Calvin Klein. His British Home
Stores pants are just fine; OK, even C&A –

he breathes and isn't married after all.
He can live in a kennel for all I care,
as long as his scrotum is in a state of

good repair. No money, no problem – all
I want to count is his first million sperm.
Now, if *he* finished with the fags – Oh, no,

he's the brain of a drain. Far too good-looking
anyway, must be gay. And what's worse,' she says,
'I'm beginning to feel sisterly with that sinister spider,

you know, fertilised it kills the male, eats him
before things get stale. I'm already drawn
to wearing black. And aren't men like applecores,

after you've extracted the seeds? I'm a chick,
all right, warming up her eggs. Do you think if
I just explained to one about how I feel my meter's

running out and all he'd have to do is lie and think
of football, film stars, anything he likes – you know,
I'd even have it in a bag, provide pictures like a clinic;

these days a re-usable syringe, kinda hard and squirty,
begins to look as sexy as a plastic-coated penis feeling
flirty. In fact,' she continues, 'If only sperm was spurted

on the National Health – I'd even pay a Single Supplement
for every go – I wouldn't have to beg or be polite, bother
with all that white wedding shite, wouldn't have to modernly

pretend I don't want babies for *years* – if *ever*.'
And after seven glasses of cheapish Chardonnay,
she slurs: 'You know, if sperm was on prescription,

all we'd need is a brief description. I could kill
that Mills and Boon infection – silly ideas of "him"
that cling. In fact, with *him*. Wouldn't that be revenge

for trying to make us insect thin?' Funny, as she
stuffs a puffy cushion up her fluffy mohair jumper,
black, and sighs, she seems to have multiple eyes.

Egg and Sperm Meet

Egg welcomes desperate sperm.
I see both a child's school diagram –
compass circle, mad tadpole
cheery-tailed, almost giggling –
and television picture, popular
science, camera fine as a butterfly
feeler; the sperm in nature's
winning vest gets the big mama
egg, burying its head
as if in a single breast.
Spent. And I see cells,
dividing like bubbles,
one into two and so on,
until an eye, thigh; hand
holding. Gut-punching miracles.
But why is what escapes,
I hunt. Where is the spark –
invisible, mysterious, God.

INSIDE, NOT ME

An anemone pulse of fingers, blood, and magic

Scan

In me a moonscape of organs,
bloodless, maybe a monster;

my blood thuds. Until a black
bubble. Silent, slow as a flower,

opening from limb buds,
an anemone pulse of fingers.

Under my thick skin veil,
not me, plugged; blind,

bulb-headed, spinning invisible
tissue on bones fine as fish.

Mouse-big, sparrow-hearted,
it becoming *you*, new from

nothing; the miraculous alien,
eel-supple in blank dreams.

And like men loving the blue
planet, the world is changed.

Baby Pattern

What pattern so advanced
it seems to me magic,
locked invisibly in vacant air,
herds the teeming cells accurately
into an eye, heart, hand.

I want to kneel that this is possible.

To feel the power to paint, write,
hear music, and know these only
ghosts – raindrops to a storm.

The Good Thing about Being Pregnant . . .

*Ante-natal class question: What are the good things
about being pregnant?*

Leaving out the baby, of course, the only good thing
about being pregnant is that workmen in the street
no longer shout obscenities, or tell you to cheer up.
After so many years of seeing them in the distance
like unavoidable exams, what sweet relief.

And feeling mighty vulnerable, I discover
unexpectedly that I have power. Frightened
or embarrassed by my stomach, they avert
their eyes. No, *Fancy a shag? Have you not
got a smile?* (No matter if your father's on
his deathbed, your 17-year-old dog's gone
blind, or your sanitary towel needs changing.)
I could finally get revenge – what if I walked
up now and shouted, *Show us your dick then!
Give you one!* And if he says anything sassy
back – *Are you a poof?*
Don't make me relent by sweeping quickly the street
of trippable chips, saying something kind. What's
wrong? Can you see me now as your girlfriend;
your sister, your daughter, your mother, your wife?

Gene Soup

Colour photos always show the night and day
shades of our hair, and skin, magnolia and gypsy.

Our Celtic eyes are closer. Sea moods. But I would
choose your uncanny cat green, curtain tassel lashes,

so useful for a boy, if I had the luxury of not worrying
about deformity. Our mouths should guarantee Cupid

bows, but maybe that ignorant holiday wine a cleft palate,
hare lip. Your surfacing skeleton, my marshmallow hips –

how could any artist blend us in his palette? But boiling
in the bladder-stirred dark, I see gene soup; brilliant DNA

like fairy lights, linked like primary school children's paper
chains. A turmoil of dropped beads. Re-strung by hands I cannot

see, a pristine pattern made from us. With all that we have
seen and felt, rubbed out, erased, like acid-bathed bones.

Mrs Smug

Mrs Smug hasn't felt sick. *I've been so lucky,*
so well, she smirks smugly – I could have puked
on her. Mrs Smug hasn't swollen; witch-thin chin,
ankles like sparrows', promised glossy locks from
hormones that can sometimes leave you greasy.
Guess which I got. Spots too. She blooms. I balloon.

Mrs Smug doesn't worry: *Pregnancy and parenthood,*
it's just natural; all you have to do is go with it, she says
in her most encouraging voice, beaming warm as a strip-
light. You can smell her confidence at the ante-natal class,
strutting in the air, laughing at the nagging of the rest
of us's neuroses. *You just have to be positive.* Grrrr.

Mrs Smug tells the class, especially the single mother,
of how perfectly her husband hubs. *Oh, so supportive.*
In fact, he knows so much, can breathe and push,
he could practically have the baby himself – ha, ha.
He chose the world's most boring names; she glories
in his ingenuity. Mrs Smug is as proud as punch, rubbing
in her silly status to the mum who's unemployed, of a job
that makes me feel snobby – she deserves a punch.

Mrs Smug has the nursery painted, sleepsuits bought,
cot sheets folded. Her route is decided, her bag all packed,
down to the offputting cushion of vast maternity pads.
She scores full points in the *How Prepared Are You?*
quiz; the class confers but can't quite catch her.

Mrs Smug has no pain in her back – she's a pain in the neck.
No indigestion, heartburn, excessive weight gain. No urges
for cakes, sweety binges – nothing strange. *A healthy diet
is best for baby*, she says. She makes my narcolepsy worse.

But when it's all over, a class reunion. She brings
him in his prim Mary Poppins pram; I peer in and
secretly smirk. I mean, no baby is ugly, but . . .

My Belly Blossoms

Trees bleed. Oozing berries,
branch clots hanging, spotting
earth's lumpen brown skin.
Spattered where veins burn
green to red on the pavement
plastering of leaves, flat as stamps.

Deep snowdrop seed mumbles, sleepy –
*Our first bloodless white lips will kiss
the empty cradle.* But most nuts, pods,
bulbs, seeds, swell sympathetically
as my belly blossoms. Bones like birds',
fish skeleton spine in there, brain florets,
limb stubs, eyes for God's sake – human
soup. The immaculate stir of cells secret
as sucking waterlily roots in the dark
for future plump buds.

But mysteries of mind swim still; even
this baton of life, fuse we lit in my own
host body world does not unfog the prickling
stars of understanding. Ignorant as a flower,
all I know is in spring will be a hill of skin,
strung drum bald; bursting.

Finding and Joining With Father-To-Be

What chemical promptings,
spiritual perfumes leaking

through the eyes; which
fantastic pattern – place, age,

decision, ribbon of time.
Which brain-urged words

slipping from the flowering
mouth, *To kiss soon I must,*

led us to this dark dreaming
in our nest, with our compass

of eyes, face, hands, feet and
hair, mapping the possible.

What Does it Feel Like?

But what does it <u>feel</u> like, girlfriends
say, as I did; a baby inside, new life?

Nothing at first. Only knowing something lurks
in the dark like a ghost in a bedroom. Surely
there should be a sign, a word on my forehead,
announcement by angels, heavenly choir. But
only dumb breasts feeling punched, vomiting, tell.

Then I'm waiting for 'butterfly flutters', anxious at night,
easily mistaken, so warns the book, for uneasy food. But
I've felt the cobalt crash, a Moor Blue burring on my cheek,
no, this sensation is of a slight internal breeze, ruffling
of water, barely there; the amoebas' transparent dance. Becomes
an oily ripple, vaguely disturbed sea, more than a swell.
I feel like a throat sweet, liquid in the middle, as if the moon
might suck me like a wave. Then squirming – a minnow captured
in a skin jar – and finally a big fish, an exercising salmon in a too
small pool. My insides feel like when you push your hand through
moving water from a boat. I think: I wish I hadn't seen *Alien*.

Then limbs, fists, feet – not fins for sure, which couldn't kick
like this or punch ribs as if a cage of bones, inanimate.
To be kicked from the inside out turns the world weird; topsy-turvy –

I'll find flowers looking at the grass, sky drowning in the sea,
sun inking day with black light. Now I know as if I've seen
a photograph – an out-of-focus face, a blur of hair – there is a baby,
a human in there. But not enough to shyly speak, choose suitable
music as you should.

The sense of strangeness never goes, that inside another person
grows, of otherness contained within the self, a magic that the male
can never share, nor even all the women asking the question
like I did: *What does it feel like?*

It feels something like . . . harbouring events massive as
the planet orbits, understanding infant stars, the start
of spring, birds' winter arrowing. Why abundant Earth was born
from dust and gas, in blackness. Knowing why the moon rocks
the sea; and time folds like a handkerchief. Like being the sun for
Earth. Light for leaves. As immense.

Blood Tests

Always we thought, without question, discussed,
how it would not be kind to bear a baby afflicted,
wronged in nature, but when Dracula tubes suck
my blood for scientists to read Latin words written
in the red, I have witnessed the flutter beat of my
seahorse-curled foetus, heard *Baby* in my head.

Take this cup from me, I saw myself praying as needles
invaded my vein, sniffed blood. I practically had stigmata,
just thinking with the company of stars, of deciding. Who
draws the line, tells bravery must be mine, not poor being's,
powerless, in the dark. I think in particular of when we're dead.
No angels brought answers. I just saw myself praying –
Take this cup from me.

How could I kill you, although still the size of my little finger,
like an insect, imperfect; inside I can feel you, I've seen you alive.
Fate, don't make me. How could I survive that type of death
and live. How could I let you live if I love you, and already I do –
inside I can feel you, I've seen you alive – if you cannot live with
dignity, any pleasure ever. How could I leave you if I did, when I
die, to the vagaries of strangers, if your body is ugly, same baby
brain. *What if nobody cuddled you ever again?*

Feeling Round

I am a child's drawing,
a circle on stick legs;
the Spacehopper I had.

My skirts sit like Saturn rings –
try fitting knickers on an apple,
tights on a tortoise. What if
my head proves heavier than my legs,
in the public swimming pool; I'm stuck
upturned like a beached sheep?

I'm an earth mother all right –
same size and round. I assume
my pubes – don't miss them much
though. Not like my waist, that mourned
curve, boned, deflated feet, twinless chin.

I'm so sorry, body,
that I ever complained
about any of you at all,
now that I have the figure
of a large beachball.

The Only Mother-To-Be

Am I the only mother-to-be who worries about a monster
and the terrible wounding love of it. Womb dark so blind –
bathroom glass scans showing only blurred, limbed fish,
alien heads. Am I the only one who fears in the long vomit
mornings, urine-urgent night, tomato-tight skin. A split.
How juicy inside. And the blood, arteries waving like plug-
torn wires. Dying like a Victorian on white sheets.

Imagine shitting a football, my earthy friend says, but
it's not pain I mind, it's being 'torn', which makes you
sound like paper, but every woman knows her skin,
prim, pursed sphincter, would never tear clean, but
like a green branch, very messy. Or the baby's head
might stick, a wine cork you can't push back in – defects,
damage, death. Or health, perfection, happiness. Wait,
woman, in between, ride nightmare and dream like a
legs-apart cowgirl. How can bunnies, bows distract?

A Bigger World

My heart is your sun,
my blood air, food.

You float in me like Columba
in his coracle of skin;

I am your sea, walking
I rock you like waves.

I am your diving bell,
you explore on a rope

of oxygen. Shellfish
limbless you swim

until hand and foot buds
open anemone slow,

to knock, already wanting
the shore of a bigger world.

NEW HUMAN

Puzzled by light, air, touch, love

Caesarean

As if shocked, hypothermic, joking but my knowing body
trembles, I wait, a line in my spine like a vein of melting
ice – pain-killing fluid that has coolly nearly killed me.

The operating theatre smells like hell one open door away.
It can't be me, this local anaesthetic part, I'm too squeamish
to be conscious – an operation live performed behind a crude
chest curtain. Eye to horrified eye, husband, we huddle scared
as children under covers, mouthless green monsters outside.

Lights! The costumes are right, just like ER, Casualty,
modernised MASH – bring in Dr Ross, Hawkeye, kind
Mike Barratt. But these are strangers doing a job, a *job*
which takes a secret scalpel to my sealed skin, trusting
numb abdomen, cuts the thin white epidermis, fat fat,
mother-of-pearl muscles and nerves I imagine now as
damaged filigree too delicate to mend, imagining hard
then elsewhere, anywhere, like the dentist's chair, times
ten. So close, husband, eye to eye, as if a person's single
pair. I remember how grateful, glad I was that you were
you, married to me, that you would never leave, even
now as they opened my body and your nervous, nauseated
forehead sweated. I forget why I am there, just endure the
trail of time until below the bending heads, as if they wrestle,

rummage in my tummy with a possessed hot water bottle.

Strange, I think.

Then there is a baby. In the air.

Grey-blue, squeezed from his drained pool,
amazed in a big Sister's scrubbed arms. Surreal.

He is brought to my head, grimacing
like a gorgeous gargoyle – puzzled
by light, air, touch, love.

After the Caesarean

Thumb-pumping for pain,
I self administer morphine,
so high now in 'High Dependency'

I laugh alone at the name play.
I need sleep, but can't stop looking –
there is a *baby*! A baby in a blanket

in a clear plastic cot – hygienically
hospital-wrapped. At my side –
he's *mine*! Is it illusion?

If I shut my eyes the best hallucination
I could dream might vanish from this
drugged dawn, leave me more alone

than I could ever bear again. My river-
dreaming cactus lips prickle, can only
suck ice-cubes from a nurse's palm –

swallowing diamonds slippery as fish
in my line-free hand, welcome as nectar,
they melt into wine. Now we float

in struggling colour, a Chagall, mother and baby
high as stars over the sleeping world, bumping
into smiling angels. I'm the sole patient, patient.

It is silent, even the distant scribbles
of the crisp kind nurse in her dove hat –
but heart music, universal, *fortissimo*.

The Caesarean Wound

Don't feel a failure, I'm told –
natural birth, a vaginal delivery
isn't everything. But I don't.

I can even laugh at my innocent
pills – homeopathic, organic,
with pictures of hills; my flower

remedies, aromatherapy oils –
(proved not essential, like morphine) –
mood music, candles, breathing book.

I feel cut. Pulled tight together again
by ingenious plastic wire and beads,
like a drawstring bag. Harvested.

Five layers, I'm told, below the sheep
shorn mound to the deeply private womb,
all stitched now with agonising care.

Big drugs drip into my veins, sicken;
I am punctured punctually. I feel like
a fixed garment, invisibly mended but

never the same again. Marked. But when
I look, swallow the horror I've been so split,
I am pleased. So thin the incision, smiling

at me with its curved ruby lip. So bloodless.
Already you can see how hair will grow
like weeds healing dug earth wounds.

Midwives

Emergency. They come like doves on thrown bread;
starchy wingish rushing on rubber-soled, whispering
white shoes. Drugged, they are easily angels, anchor

hands in hormonal storms, feet of earth. Their names,
and nursery nurses too, more beautiful than chance –
Miranda, Flora, Oona, Senga . . . and others faded into

flowery vowels, sweet syllables, only saying now, *Sister,
sisters.* A fortnight's faces, voices, morphine-morphing
into one, always smiling in white – the Bride of Birth,

(though labour clothes were blue suits like comfy plumbers).
They clean my blood, fix my drip and dignity, so kind I cry.
I kept thinking – *What I do is light as air compared to deep*

and salty water. I remember especially how older Flora
brushed and combed my trashed hair and pride, washed
my face and hands, tender as Jesus. I was humbled.

Suddenly a Baby

Brain-spraining, Dali-strange, in a stranger's bare arms,
suddenly a baby. (*Nothing else, not a carrot or a lamb;
a radio, a hat. Not nothing because it's all been a mistake,*

just air.) A grey baby as the book foretold, pink coming,
a closed rose bud. Like wings, lungs unfold in oxygen.
Our harmonious cord cut, Sister brings him like a prince

to his admiring people – a sedan of hands. Expressions
rehearse fast as flames when first I look into my baby's face;
calm like evening-ironed water. Light-shy eyes try, winks

of white and bleeding blue like Victorian Willow unearthed.
My mind is crashing like a computer, but I see creation
in skin; I understand Jesus. I see the hand of God as

clearly in the tiny ones as stamped *Made in Hong Kong.*

Hospital Nursery

New humans mew,
shrink-wrapped in blankets,
loud as lost lambs.

Extra-terrestrials longing
for home, the warm
dark water planet

that rocks, rumbles,
thuds; protects.
Jolie-laides,

the beautiful uglies squirm,
faces like ancient adults
sucking sour plums.

A refugee protest –
fists of angry red
fingers punch alien air.

Blue Poppies

Violet eyelid-veined, orange-throated, blue poppies
with emaciated purple stars pinned at neck and shy head
as if buttonholed for their own wedding with water sounds –
water necklaces of glassed white pebbles, strung on clear
twisted liquid strings, slipping from the midget hill like saliva-
shone peppermints into the pool's slavering lips that sing tunelessly,
endlessly of garbled stone and water, water eating stone slowly by
licking like lollipops of toddlers – and sun. Wearing themselves
like large-brimmed, wind-saucering hats. From China, Papaveraceae,
they bow, loose yellow tongues slobering pollen, wasteful as
goldsmiths' dust, onto blue, royalled petals startling as summer sky
tissue cut into floaty flower shapes; God's craft class. Cool water
shades to their Communist red relations burning in the fields.

And like a delicate skeletal hand in rough fur gloves, an elegant
woman's unexpectedly hairy leg, slim stem, rabbit ear leaves,
are bristled, bold, like a red-haired man's five o'clock chin,
aggressive ginger halo. The haired pods are totally male, seeded.

Wind moves blue poppies like Scotland's saltires, foreigners
in the new exotic public garden. The new blue-eyed baby looks
at them and they look back like more blue eyes of earth – also
fresh to the surface, dazzling air.

A BABY

This hand, Bonsai, clutches my heart

The Good News

If you didn't have to be divine, could hire disciples,
I'd take a dozen, send them to the edges of the earth
to tell my good news – (relatives first, of course).

If I hadn't been born in the 20th century (and it wasn't
wet and wild and windy), I'd light a beacon on a hill
like at Pagan Beltane, and watch my brilliant message,

written in the rapid languages of fire, spark across
the land, jump into space. Look, even the twinkle-
sending dead, stars, hear, jitter in their sockets,

trying to get warm, get happy. Instead, I burn
my urgent tongue, heat my ear, with telephone
breath, rush to the rainy window, suddenly

sun-blinded – there must be words shining
on the line, strung like wet web's silver beads,
hung like bunting: flowers bursting from a branch.

Baby Hand

Not bones but muscular air
inside; why starfish spread
five doll small living fingers
with cushion button dimples
for knuckles. All of you
shocks me with wonder,
but in particular this hand,
Bonsai, clutches my heart,
hurts. With unlikely strength
squeezes my eyes without
mercy as it pairs and prays
in the yellow curtain-warmed
dawn; coils my bird perch
pinky like the spring tendrils
of the Morning Glory.
Palm pads pressure – a punch
from a pussy willow – a half
inch lifeline in their fresh creases.
Go on, grow, long as a plane
trail, as shining, but let me stay
more – gripped by miracle.

Blessed

Softly volcanic, this soul glory, brimming
to mouth and eyes – spilling it should be white
like thickened light, with water nature. I am
a Renaissance scene, a Madonna, a pale Raphael,
in a state of such grace I half expect to see angels
standing on star shoes in the window's small sky,
the same glory pouring from their open mouths,
then sailing down on swan wings, doves opening
like flowers from their hands, to look with cobalt
eyes on the baby born. *Life*, they choir, painting
angels day-lighting night, pointing incandescent
ET fingers – *Life from nothing, safe – rejoice*!

His Round Skull

Round, my fruit's ripe skull, uncrushed;
unsquashed, unwrinkled skin. No birth

struggle – a lift into bright air. No fighting
pubic bones, suffocating tunnel flesh. From

moment one, head perfect, cranium plates
just kissing cerebellum-sheltering membrane

over the disturbing fontanelle pulse. No bruises
purpling. Ball angles. Firm on the white neck stalk.

No part in the drama; trauma did not mark,
mould the world. Blanket-gathered, laid in

a woven Moses basket, my womb's first
harvest – let such calm seed his years.

Baby Foot

Monkey-curling in my palm,
a whole foot with more room.
Polished sole snow would sand;
white nail moons shine
in pea-pod neat rows of toes
tinier than my teeth.
My muckle thumb irons
smiling ankle folds
in marshmallow skin;
no bones poke.
Ball, heel, arch
in perfect mini replica,
like those joke shoes
pretend this happy foot
only fit for walking on air
might ever weigh Earth
with heavy brain
or heart –
no longer stepping safe
in my harmless giant's hand.

What Have I Ever Done So Good

What have I ever done so
good to deserve a baby.

I am on my knees in park blossom,
shoving flowers in my milk-moist
mouth, kissing cherry petals pink

and white as unsunned skin, essence
of baby snow crowding in my eyes –
the poppy concert opposite. Will I

lick these sticky buds exploding after
slow tree sex into row on row of small
green flags everywhere welcoming

my little one, deafening the pin-head
larks. But I'm not mad on Spring's drug –
though I sprint through grass with lamb limbs,

it's those trying, crying in my heart now –
wanting loud as the dry Moon coping
always with her round eyeful of Earth.

Thank You Prayer

I have no words for my *Thank You* prayer;
none are long enough or big enough, and
happiness's interference, like the airwaves'

white noise, keeps hijacking my mind's silence.
I am a child at Christmas who can't sleep, except
I have what I want; a dog fussing his master home,

wind-mad leaves escaped from their tree. I even pose
like a praying person, pious as a painting, reminding
myself it's hardly fair to only pray when everything

is bad – how boring for God, how utterly depressing,
(though much easier to remember). But at last I must
rush to the park, lie flat on the grass, roll around like

a sow in hairy green mud. I kiss a flower smiling at me
from the earth – it's spring after all, they'll just think
I'm lamb-daft. But really I'm confident of God

hearing the good grammar of gladness,
emotion's untrained eloquence –
the unlying language of the heart.

Wonder

Never have I felt the word *wonder* properly until now.
The Northern Lights on a stoned night, Thai temples
incense-dim with emerging mountainous gold Buddhas,
Greenland's rippled white hide from dizzy air, swollen
suns engorging further with autumn light, a turquoise-
chambered winter sky fireworked with shooting stars.
Frost chasing the skeleton of everything, furring trees with
sparkling sleeves – on and on from memory's glory stores.

But even these passed away, printing only a shining
in the mind like the blinded retina's wound of light.
Everything except you. I maintain a wonder state,
a feeling peak, an endless spine-stroking string on a
climactic high violin, the laughing madness of first love,
an always darkless dawn in a season-stalled spring. *No,*

there is nothing to compare with just looking, looking
at my new human who came out of nothing perfectly
toed and fingered with bowed rose lips, surprised eyes
and the ghost of our faces miraculously in his face
like those Madonnas blooming improbably in stone.

Can my soul take the strain, this constant bubbling
in the brain; will my wings incinerate in a spontaneous

combustion of the heart? *No.* These are the supreme weeks
of living, face to small face with creation. Wonder inside
everywhere like water, a drug, erupting from my skin's pores,
my mouth and hands, my baby-mirrored eyes; like the sun's
surface, lava. Like cousin love it multiplies, harmlessly keeps
high; in these dying summer afternoons solidifies to happiness,
like wax cooling into candles, haloes around my baby and me.

Another Mother and a Pram

Bumble bees bump on air above,
purring as busy bitter wasps
whine, pattable furry stripes
lost in their bird-big silhouettes
against a heart-blinding blue sky.

Pigeons gargle music, puff
paradise breasts burnished
by brassy sun. Pond ducks,
AWOL, walk clumsily as seals.
I hear fat buttery daffodils
kissing their reedy spines.

Flat on the grass, I know
my weeks old baby breathes
in his portable nest, here.
I see myself to park walkers
passing, another mother
and a pram. Can they not
see happiness fizzing like
a firework from my eyes;
around me like a brilliant gas?

My Baby's Hands

That scanned star
of certain fingers,
waving underwater slow
in the sealed dark windowed;
the truth of you being alive,
human, free as a kite
in a tide-pulled sky of water.

Then doll-small in summer's
blurry night light laid,
praying without God thoughts
or words on milking mouth.
No pores puncture skin
where air is rough,
adult pads sand.

I hold your curled baby hands
fresh as unfurled leaves;
know I'll hold as long
as I breathe, beat – no,
even when my own
are only bone.

I Am a Mummy

I am a mummy!
I am a mummy!
I am a mummy!

My heart shouts
in its singing voice
only kept for happy
thoughts like *Spring*,
the leaping of *Love*.

Grown up little girl
dreaming adult games,
the blood reminder;
but impossible still
this egg and sperm race.

These sucking lips,
pouty as a fish,
will call me mummy.
My tummy thrills –
I am a *mummy*!

Breast-feeding

Limpet lips, O'd as a goldfish. Human joey, foal,
kitten, puppy, piglet. Frantic for nipple, hunting
air, like slow flowers sun. First lip-dropped drips
thrill – umbilical milk, gin blue like skimmed,
hidden body skill, new woman product – *my*
milk. Female, sow, bitch, nanny, vixen, cow.
Cow content with kind milk chemicals after learner's
crab stabs made us cry, both stoned, blissed, baby
drunk into sleep, small hours. The very face of fulfilment.

Vampiric on thin women, fatter-than-blood milk.
Minerals, vitamins, they give – hair, nail, teeth, skin.
But his hunger is mine – I eat mountains, am swollen
as a river. Sex squeezes, drains from these bare
breasts, forgotten their ballgown impertinence,
racy black lace; now nun innocent, uncupped,
blobbing from big lifting industrial bras, thick
elastic straps. But night illuminates their white,
dimly luminous at dawn, his soft paws laid there,
sweet. He primes the mummy pump, silent
pulsing sucks until drugged. Plugged and
unplugged, I am food, drink, everything.

Crying

1
I am crying too, curiously with dry eyes –
sobs choke stomachs, tears release – because
it will not stop and the time before of silence
or orderly sound is a *must* memory like water.

The tenement twists in its dark bandage of sheets –
soon the whole world will hold its billion billion
hands to eggshell heads. The sea bed cracks –

waves shuddering, reined, sucked down, drowned
into flat water. Planets scatter like snooker balls,
moon lurches, stops her hauling of reluctant seas,
covers dusty ears before she crumbles. Sun hides
behind the dirty blanket of the early hours – tell-tale
light leaking here and there. Flowers dive brownly
into earth, wishing themselves seed. In Africa, animals
stampede. Let me drink, swim in soundlessness,
like an atom; transparent amoeba. Noise wasps swarm
in my brain – a body of glass bones, ping-pong ball
skull, egg eyes, petal skin in my vibrating arms.

I beg you, Your Smallness, I am your slave always,
you know; I give, do, say, sing, anything. O Tiny

Tyrant, your willing servant suffers so. Step on her
with your inch long lily feet – only have mercy.

2
At night crushing silence louder than the peace
of granny stars, clouds big as houses sailing,
jump-leads to our brains, interferes with inner ear –

helmets of skull hopeless. B-movie zombies rise,
thumping of blind legs begins. Eyes look punched.
I will not allow this noise – as if my lamb laments

the whole world's endless woes, the black television
children – to wire me up, I say. Why this pressing
of temples then, to defend my mind from a new

violence of sound? Why these red moments then,
blood rage, fading to purple, brain bruises?
I am a tin toy, key being tighter tighter turned –

without will, I will burst into action, star in a horror
film, wind at the edge tearing my hair; gloving
fingers with wicked power, inking hearts, and nobody,
not even me, would understanding the plot, losing it.
Let *fuck* be enough – I can rinse out my mouth with baby
soap. Fuck, fuck, *shut the fuck up!* There.

Baby Pose

That splayed teddy leg spread,
like when I learned to swim –
Be a frog, still supple in the hip.

A freshly unfolded foetus fall
of bowed thighs, jewelled
with genitals, gorgeously small.

And your arms – two little L's
thrown back, fists fit to punch
a butterfly balled bud tight.

All else is thrown open,
even the skull's soft fontanelle,
unbearable trust exposed;

except the secrets
of your sealed mind,
stirring under milk whimpers.

My Baby Breathing

No mouth sound, cloud colouring,
such frail air vanishing in transparent air;

I want wind. Months of water – learn,
merman. Look, dolly chest – heaving

breast hills, hurricane lungs – that won't puff
champing dandelion seeds. I eat my heart again;

a mouse beats bigger. Black-eye tired,
my vigil blinks in dangerous sleep.

Open – show me night eyes, blue, blurry
as sea's winded waves; twitch starry hands,

twinkle toes, just stir – take all
my expert breaths for one more.

Baby in the Daffodils

We plump you in a flock of daffodils,
a migration on stalks, a common motion,

earth's blonde spring hair ruffled
by affectionate wind. *Yes, yes, yes,*

they agree. *Yes, yes, yes,* madly
nodding. *We love your baby,*

he is more like us than you. New.
Our buds unfurl like fresh fingers

petals soft as skin; his blood is clear
as sap, he has our colouring,

yellow curls, sky in his eyes,
cheeks blowing. They bend

over you like anxious aunties,
all kissing at once. You grab

a hooked green throat,
stuff its open golden mouth

into your own tight rose.
With two teeth and cat's

tongue you eat a flower,
smiling like a young god

accustomed to nectar.
How they laugh hysterically

en masse, indulgently shining
in your face like sun.

Inhaling his Hair

I inhale my baby's
dandelion hair –

failed fingers, cheeks,
envy nose and air

feeling white filaments
finer than the burn

of snow on skin,
clumsy dust crashing,

swans' rough wings.
An aroma of clouds,

sun scent, in this summer
aureole, seeded scalp.

BEING HUMAN
IS ENOUGH IN COMMON

Fat, Christmas, and ghosts of nightgown

My Stomach After

Deflated after drumskin months –
balloon burst, pod split, packed
space vacated – that mirror moment.

I inhale big, but see my stomach sagging
like an old sow, that Japanese pot-bellied
pig we laughed at in the zoo. A plastic bag

billowed by its shoulders in a windy tree.
Blind at least to its smiling wound, I sit
for shock; it sits slightly on my lap – *How*

d'ye do, I'm new! I feel like a let down tent,
made from Tesco's Own Bakery whole day's
dough, it looks like a tub of raspberry ripple;

a Slimmer of the Year's discarded garment.
Why is a woman's stomach not designed
to stretch for babies' bums, heads, lengths?

If you'd bought it you'd return it to the shop –
faulty, doesn't fit, has marked. Permanently.
Over-stretched-elastic muscles moan, girn

at every move. How much aerobics did I do
before? I could have stuck to sofa surfing,
armchair athletics – The Lost Remote, Crisp

Sprint, Marathon Marathon, Wine Time Trials.
Is this evolution's cruel idea of a fair exchange?
To break my hourglass, pump my tum, waste

my waist – leotards and high leg pants, midriff
tops, hipsters and bikinis, for my big baby's beauty?
OK.

Pram Rage

Onward in our chariot, baby, Ben Hur, in the evening-ghosted streets. Fast white wheels luminous, hardly seeming to touch ground, except on cobbles which make you giggle, like pigeon explosions in the park.

But in the day town we are slowed, a wing-clipped bird, by legs and feet frequent as weeds and more irritating – excuse me, *excuse me*, EXCUSE ME! But a pram has made my words loud as mouthing fish, and what's more, the secret of invisibility has been discovered by my pram, despite its brightly coloured hide – model 'chameleon' obviously. Trip, bump, then tuck at *me*! *Bash my scarcely sleeping baby's head with that fat bag and I'll rip you limb from limb, sir.*

And at doors, why do people assume that I shall wait and wait and wait while a babbling stream of shoppers pass on through – it's never *my* turn. And while I'm on the subject, why does the whole of humankind, except other mothers, even young feminists, presume me stupid, slow, second class, just because I push a pram? Do degrees, high professions, just plain brains, competence, experience and talent, strangers' manners, vanish, just because you've given birth? And does it make you deaf? – *A leopard-skin changing bag and mat, how very strange. Is that a BOY in a pink hat? (Gasp!) People shouldn't bring these pushchairs into shops* . . . What would you suggest, bovine madam? My baby sails, flies? My family go naked, starve now we are three, and stay indoors as punishment for having the next generation which will pay your pension . . . *Maybe,* my baby says – if he could.

And OK, maybe I have got milky, splashy stains on my top like a Florence statue, an odd sock, my hair is far from advert fresh. Maybe I have too many bags bulging from my pregnant pram and my hungry baby is girning until the next breast-feeding place distant as Everest, but must you look at me in that 1950s way as if I was a failure as a mother, and a person. Piss off! It's hard but I'm happy.

I imagine a protest, all of us on wheels, prams and wheelchairs en masse in the main street; we clog the doors of shops, let doors slam (revengefully) in startled faces, swarm slowly over stairs demanding lifts and where there are some, push in front and fill, create escalator hell – that'll teach'em to appreciate the choice, lazy gits. I see us weaving back and forth like fences round the wheel-less, aware only of ourselves, clipping heels and glaring if they complain. But we kiss all those who respect and help us in our struggle, especially with steps.

In the meantime – just until I've time, I mean, my husband buys a pushbike bell and mounts it on the handlebar. A cardiac effect – see them scatter in the street, like rabbits foxed, hee, hee. I half expect to see us on the news – *In the first confirmed case of pram rage* . . . so many altercations have there been, but I feel like a pioneer of wheels in a square world, a humble but important offshoot of the Suffragettes. To all parents, I say, join the cause – *Push Your Pram With Attitude!*

Watchnight Service

You slept still as the straw-snug Jesus doll,
white hat halo, tinselled for a laugh – churchyard
breaths not big enough to cloud pincered air.

Latecomers already saw you, smiling wide whisky-
softened smiles, perfume of Laphroaig lingering
after peering in the pram, laughing too loudly at
the plastic Made-in-China star on the pram handlebar.

The glow of old carols, bone candles, music hurrying
from the organ's thin silver throats to midnight;
the Christmas tree grins, heating sharp needles
in its garish Pagan dress, gaudy necklace of lights.
Without crying, quietly, you waken. Radiant
lampshade skin, wild hay hair, egg-blue eyes;
you raise gold arms like a Raphael, Evangelist,
coo dove-in-the-sun croons as if rehearsed.

Word spreads, flat backs turning into faces. For each
a smile that irons the crumpling of years, until even
the minister, eagled in his lonely pulpit looks, catches
joy – what anyone would wish for Christmas. Bells jump.

'The child is born; he is among us,' he says.

Nature's Censor

I could use an erect penis for a hat peg.
In all the bits for schoolboy rudeness,
double-entendres, the hot fumbling,
slippery, sucking, murderous power

of sweaty sex, noosed with the stupid
pulsing heart, a metamorphosis. Nature's
censor. My Page Three breasts are filled
with innocents' milk – (*Whoar! Give us*

a drink, darlin'. Mine's a pint.) I'll be a cow
if you squeeze – an exclusive on kissable nipples
for my baby's little lips. Just the words 'birth
canal' – a vision of a baby captaining a barge,

a spyglass in his hand. He flies the Jolly Roger,
pirating my husband's private place. My stomach
has a flapping apron like a matron, my thighs
sigh on seats, bottom hangs in shame. But our

bed blossoms with love, extravagantly pure
as the cherry, our baby between us.

First Look

From an underwater-blurred world,
milky bliss or bawling milkless hunger,

nestled shawl-warm or naked
in uncaring bloodless air,

your restless sea-colour eyes,
sequinned with bedside light,

focus on my face.
A first look.

Your thin forehead skin
crinkles like clingfilm –

hello, confused human,
apprentice person.

Look, stay hooked
on my pupil; learn,

these features always
mean love – it's *me*.

Sleeping with Baby

Let a baby in bed and you'll
never get it out, people say.

Between us, he is us. The seam,
the impossible join I had dreamed
to defeat death chilling one, the other
still warm, beating, too sad.

Would animal mummies of snuffling hungry puppies,
fluffy-footed, sapphire-eyed kittens, Bambi-spotted,
eye-lashed fawns, lambs wet as hand-washed wool,
banish them at night, needlessly, as orphans, from their
warm flanks and huge bell hearts? Barbarian behaviour,
humans. We are a family, lying content as fed lions
in the borrowed feather heat of our tidy duvet nest,
knowing our animal. And whatever trouble, tears
cloud the future like condensation on a window,
nothing would make me miss the upturned sniff
of your snaily nose, your fish-full lips falling apart
like a rose, sleeping marble eyes, horizontal aureole
of hair exploring my cheek gentle as Star Moss
searching for a home in stone; my revelling in rows
of five toes, clutching bunches of fiddly tiddly fingers.

Sometimes I can't sleep for being glad, my smiles
blooming in the dark, extra stars. I dare to stroke your
puppet-poised hands, womb-bent legs, lily skin – new
blood bounces my heart redder, fuller, an attack of love.
I kiss your temple like a priest, closing my eyes because
I am blessed. You stir with the sweetest mini sound,
milk-white flowers in your breath. Gently, I untouch.

You roll into me like the sausage game, snuggle as if skin
were air, water, something permeable; wanting inside, back
to that first small happy dark, thwarted by a fence of ribs.
My bones stiffen until dawn. How can I move; sometimes
I can't sleep for fear – crushing, suffocation. How much wine
is drunk? Of unsupportable burden. Sometimes I jolt awake,
my heart bleeding fear into my jumping stomach; then
struggling light shows your little ghost of nightgown, chest
waves. In out, in out, in out, rocking me back to sleep.
My smile now big as the sun.

FAMILY AND THE WORLD

Green spring fists, tooth buds and sleeping bees

Bees Hospital

No sheets for sleeping bees, sick in our Bees Hospital,
only a special stone slab, always weirdly warm as if
heat entered very slow grey veins when it sunned itself
flat out; reptile becoming mammal. Pillows of moss,
lichen to lie our buzzless patients on, wings useless
as pages torn from a book, sodden cellophane opaqued

like breathed on windows, bumbles' fluff flattened,
stormed wheatfields, rosy bumbles' sunset fur
matted, fires out. With bulbous shine, summer's
slothful raindrops, warmly engorged with light,
plop heavily from season-stolen skies – a broken
necklace of water beads scattering from the throat

of the world – surprise bees lusting after buddlia,
sucking nectar eager as drunks from bottles
in brown paper, brushing wings in gentle crashes
with butterflies blooming in the bush frequent
as the pink-hearted purple flowers, black thighs
thick, richly sacked with golden pollen. Red Admirals,

Painted Ladies, Tortoiseshells, derided Cabbage
Whites too, drookit, ruined by rain, are welcome
in the Bees Hospital – Butterfly Ward, will sip

with polite precise probosci sugar and water
solution delicate as posh old powdered ladies
from translucent china cups. As smelling salts

our crude nectar acts, *Like Lazarus* we think
in our Sunday School minds as the Admirals
hoist wings on air ropes and beat, sometimes
leaving ghosts printed, glowing in their own
gorgeous dust I know from *World of Wonder*
is made of scales, patterned, overlapped

like tiles on roofs, although you'd never guess –
maybe the roofs of Paradise. I want to gather,
harvest the precious stuff, (like wool I'm saving
when sheep leave torn clouds of rough jumpers
on barbed wire) – enough dabbed on shoulder blades
and eyes would let me join the fairies for a while,

encourage bombed bees in secret black ears,
droning in low-toned, tongue-vibrating bee language.
We must blow on them gently, just like a natural
breeze, not a lunged hurricane, human hairdryer –
Don't alarm the poor creatures, my dad said,
the bee doctor, the hospital founder who knew

when to send us like bearers of the First World
War out with our stretchers of broad green leaves

to scoop casualties from a miserable, bedraggled
death; who made it clear bees and butterflies,
their suffering, and lives mattered. Who stopped our
vintage black car, shiny, hump-backed like

the great God of Beetles, raised the bonnet
in mock breakdown to rescue balled hedgehogs
pathetically pitting hardly balloon-bursting spines
against Atlas tyres printing them to death.
We think of the cute snout sniffling, starred
black Tiggiwinkle eyes – it's ridiculously sad

to let them get squashed. And baby partridges,
pheasants fencing the road, dad capturing the last
in line with country hands to let us briefly see,
the mothers and fathers crossing calm as the Queen.
Dazzled rabbits ate lucky leaf suppers; (I wondered
if they knew and told their burrowed children, like

Watership Down). Deer would branch bald hills
again. Even wee wicked-nosed weasels sneered
respectful teeth. And adult now on grass with galaxies
of daisies, I'm anxious for the feeding bees black-
peppered at my feet, even the flowers' tutu heads,
smiley yellow eyes – who cares if people raise

eyebrows at my picking gait. And after all summer
showers I know how many bees will need hospitalised,
worry in my flat at lack of beds and staff. Soon
I will have a garden for my crawling child; but
how can I wow him with earth's casual miracles,
each bee and butterfly body, flowers breeding,

let him hatch his heart. The world itself is ill
with no space hospital big enough to heal
the earth and water, species quitting existence.
By the time this hurting tooth bud bites, wet-
mouthed, breathing forests, their men-loving
secrets, will be flames burning the eyes of God.

I still listen for the almost thrush who should be
singing from his speckled breast, soprano-puffed;
hear the silent notes from his gone beak. How can
I teach my child to suffer because the world
suffers – worse maybe than letting wet bees and
butterflies die. But also dying are the humans,

by generations slowly as individuals live. Maybe
he'll protect what's left when there are no more
bees for his hospital, no butterflies to sweetly nurse.

Can We have a Guarantee?

I thought, apart from certain eclipses of the heart
and mind, spirit hardships, I wanted to live, but

now I gobble days and Oliver-ask for more, more.
Thoughts of any theft of life, early death, tragic

family accident, squirm, curse worms in my gut,
drain my love-tamed brain. Because you need me,

need me, and even the idea of you left cuddle-less,
motherless and fatherless makes me feel mad.

Wrap us in cosmic cotton wool, bullet-proof our
hearts, lead-line our only nut-hard so hurtable heads.

Why can't we come with a guarantee, all three – free
with any family that loves each other to the point of dream.

Your Smile

I have the blood
of your smile
in my heart,

like God,
to call upon,
shine always.

Locked like the sepia
locket people
in your baby face –

like the child
my father says
still haunts me.

Learning to Stand

On the earth a stretched second
you stood, balanced. Gravity

glued dolly shoes. You wore
the sky on your head, jauntily,

light blue paper hat plumed
with feather clouds, as air's

transparent gloves cuddled
you upright. Padding paws

forgot themselves in hands.
You learn the trick of standing

as the world spins, hurtles,
turns you upside down

in darkness. Already
you'll lean less on me.

Sunny Day Prospects

How many things are better than being
in bed with my two boys, all spooned,
sleeping teaspoon goldfish-mouthed,

angel-coloured hair just touched by sun
sneaking round the heavy edges of star-
embroidered night sky curtains, their

imperfectly closed lips. It can't wait.
It's shouting in a blazing row with blue
to see who blinds best. It's pulling people

from their homes as the moon the sea,
plastering them to burning green magnetic
grass, licking white skin like an ice-cream

with blistering tongue. It's promising
flowers sweating colours, high, heady
with bee-loving perfume, that lift not

quite light as air into haloes infecting
irises of eyes. Pink lipstick lips of tarty
blushed carnations in-bred in frills, are

kissing the feet of any bees. With blue hands,
sky is drowning water's grey winter heart; wind
plays gently at shattering water mirrors, sun joins

in, agitating splinters madly like a hyperactive
child loose in granny's button box. *Get up!*
it writes with fire words new in the re-newing

mind, off by heart in the archiving heart,
hot fingers trembling at the curtain skirts.
We are ten again when it spoke with parents'

tongues, century days, the living slow,
gorgeously slow, time wasted on watchless
hands, a sweet sucked greedily but still slow,

sweetly slow. Its best trick. The baby
sleeping will today begin unwrapping
the shining wrappers of the day, inhale

the happiness, permeating gas, preserving
as amber. We will make many beads for his
human necklace. Look, we would thread

any part of us to make it charming, beautiful.
Wear our two hearts like twin roses, a garland
of days and hours glorious, complete as flowers;

kind, unthreatening as petals. We will pin
fabulous days and hours in his memory
like butterflies in a box, but they move,

flashing patterns of love. Even when dead.
He will have a drawer, runs smooth as skis
on powder, with rare eggs in his heart, a red

shining chambered drawer, those rare eggs
nestled careful, conservation species, phoenix
properties. They will hold perfect days, like

the one birds warming up their beaks like an
orchestra to announce, perfectly preserved,
contained, colour-coded and more, like seeds

their power disguised, camouflaged, the flocks
in speckled eggs in pebble nests, they will hatch
good things in him. See them hopping down

the years. See how they open their wings,
how wet feathers weather rain, open
to the sun. Open, open and happy, fly.

Baby Laugh

A bird learned human, this musical coo,
heart-stabbing sound; arrows, anchors in its
scale. We foghorn back, giants to a fairy.

Adultless comedy in fast skies, where clouds
clown, make rippling faces in creamy wind-
whipped water; winter twitches of neurotically
twisted trees; needles of rain puncturing sun's
gold autumn gut, spilling showers of phantom
leaves like fruit machines coins; the green
hysteria of park-caged spring, reaching its leafy-
sleeved arms through bars. O, to see it all still.
Remember. Let me see through your baby lenses,
contacts of joy. Unshell my brain like St Paul's
Damascus scales. Wash my windows . . . Look –

The sky widens like a smile. Earth is rolling like a ball.
The sea is dancing, cuddling the shore, wide arms
after wide arms, sweating froth like a racehorse.
The puddle of tramp's piss shimmers fit for a swan.
A dirty city squirrel smirks, laughing its lav brush tail,
spitting chips from grey lips. Muddy pig-pink chaffinches
chase and cackle, nuts for nuts. Leg-twinkling, starry-
whiskered hice mice nibble and giggle.

But funnier yet are we, stand up comics – we didn't know!
Give us a Channel 4 show! We make this flutey baby tune –
lovelier than the closing notes of a closing old orchestra,
spine-crucifying soprano – flow over and over, a spring
of fresh sounds, a world's first, important as the urgent
rush in trees' dying crowns, flamenco of flames, high thin
star noise, mosquito-fine in frost; wind screaming and
kissing – an artistic temperament, disaster and romance –
exiting animals' choir, onomatopoeic anthem, no requiem.
We hear them too, with the power of peek-a-boo.

Everything is More

Why is it with you, everything is more?
From recent crushed and bruised, cut blades,
grass blood smell is a keen green hand around
my throat, the rhododendron displays deep red
velvet whorls like cheap sex, unfurls glistening
for the sun. I must resist a public urge to hug trees –
trunks are waists drunk, welcoming. Dying daffodils
that lit your face with spring whisper to wind about
the existence of bulbs. How unbearable the sky-
rejecting willow's hang, trailing skinny fingers
in the earth like a hopeless person in a boat –
sadness twists thin wires in my juicy heart.

Paradise-breasted pigeons explode, then slide air
down again, swarming bread; a panic of ducks water-
skis back. I am in their wings light as the feather gleam,
my toes dabbling mud with lily roots. Water smoothes
over drowned trees calm as a nurse. A drug you are
in my veins, my brain – an intoxication, living supply.
You are my second chance at the world, my new blood.

Orbit of Three

Planets and stars understand
the luxury of love creating
me from my own materials
like God breathing flowers
from the seeded dust. As
abundant blue earth depends
on the sun, I am to you. You
water me. Eye-light leapt the
red boundaries of blood, stain-
glassed my heart; turned the
deaf *thud thud* counting life's
hurrying hours into drums,
duets, urging me on, on.

And we have made a moon,
out of nothing, like magicians
learning God's best trick.